HISTORY ON THE HIGH SEAS

ABOARD USS CONSTITUTION

BY THERESE M. SHEA

Gareth Stevens PUBLISHING

Please visit our website, www.garethstevens.com. For a free color catalog of all our high-quality books, call toll free 1-800-542-2595 or fax 1-877-542-2596.

Library of Congress Cataloging-in-Publication Data

Names: Shea, Therese, author.
Title: Aboard USS Constitution / Therese M. Shea.
Description: New York : Gareth Stevens Publishing, [2020] | Series: History on the high seas | Includes bibliographical references and index.
Identifiers: LCCN 2018060845| ISBN 9781538238066 (pbk.) | ISBN 9781538238080 (library bound) | ISBN 9781538238073 (6 pack)
Subjects: LCSH: Constitution (Frigate)–Juvenile literature.
Classification: LCC VA65.C7 S43 2020 | DDC 359.3/220973–dc23
LC record available at https://lccn.loc.gov/2018060845

First Edition

Published in 2020 by
Gareth Stevens Publishing
111 East 14th Street, Suite 349
New York, NY 10003

Designer: Katelyn E. Reynolds
Editor: Therese Shea

Photo credits: Cover, p. 1 Universal History Archive/UIG via Getty Images; cover, pp. 1–24 (porthole and wood background) Andrey_Kuzmin/Shutterstock.com; cover, pp. 1–24 (wood sign) ESB Professional/Shutterstock.com; cover, pp. 1–24 (brass plate) photocell/Shutterstock.com; pp. 2–24 (old paper) Kostenko Maxim/Shutterstock.com; pp. 4–24 (old notebook) BrAt82/Shutterstock.com; p. 5 DEA PICTURE LIBRARY/De Agostini Picture Library/Getty Images; p. 7 (main) NavSource Online: Service Ship Photo Archive (http://www.navsource.org/archives/09/46/46021c.htm)/Hohum/Wikipedia.org; p. 7 (Paul Revere) Museum of Fine Arts/Walk Like an Egyptian/Wikipedia.org; p. 7 (George Washington) Clark Art Institute/Scewing/Wikipedia.org; p. 9 Bettmann/Getty Images; p. 11 DEPARTMENT OF THE NAVY – NAVAL HISTORICAL CENTER/Gwillhickers/Wikipedia.org; p. 13 (main) US National Archives/Wikipedia.org; p. 13 (inset) United States Naval Academy Museum/Kaidor/Wikipedia.org; p. 15 US Naval History and Heritage Command: Photo #: NH 86692-KN/Common Good/Wikipedia.org; p. 17 Rischgitz/Getty Images; p. 19 Carpenter, Edmund J. (November 1897). "Old Ironsides". The New England Magazine XVII (3): 263-82/Lecen/Wikipedia.org; p. 21 David L. Ryan/The Boston Globe via Getty Images.

Printed in the United States of America

CPSIA compliance information: Batch #CS19GS: For further information contact Gareth Stevens, New York, New York at 1-800-542-2595.

CONTENTS

WORDS IN THE GLOSSARY APPEAR IN **BOLD** TYPE THE FIRST TIME THEY ARE USED IN THE TEXT.

COME ABOARD THE CONSTITUTION!

The USS *Constitution* is a navy vessel, or ship. "USS" means "United States Ship." This vessel was built during the early days of the United States in Boston, Massachusetts. It's a frigate, which back then was a fast warship with three masts. The *Constitution* is one of the oldest remaining warships in the world.

The USS *Constitution* was there during many important events in US history. So, come aboard and set sail on this famous vessel to learn more!

CREWMAN'S LOG

In this book, you'll read more about this ship's history from a sailor's viewpoint. While the writings in this log, or record, are made up, they're based on facts about what really happened.

USS CONSTITUTION NUMBERS

Date Launched: October 21, 1797

First Sail: July 22, 1798

Cost in 1797: $302,718

Crew in 1812: over 450 sailors

Speed in 1812: over 13 knots, or 15 miles (24 km) per hour

MORE THAN 200 YEARS AFTER ITS CONSTRUCTION, THIS NAVY SHIP IS STILL **COMMISSIONED** AND SAILING!

CONSTRUCTING THE CONSTITUTION

In the 1790s, US merchant ships needed **protection** from French ships. Congress asked that six vessels be built for this purpose. President George Washington named one the *Constitution* after the US Constitution, the highest law in the land.

Between 1794 and 1797, the *Constitution* was carefully constructed. It has very thick sides made of pine and oak. The famous **patriot** Paul Revere made metal **bolts** and other parts for it. The well-built warship would be tested in the years that followed.

CREWMAN'S LOG

We set sail on our first **mission** in 1798 and fought to protect American ships from the French. We stayed on the water 347 out of 366 days! I couldn't wait to touch the ground again!

A MAN NAMED JOSHUA HUMPHREYS **DESIGNED** THE *CONSTITUTION.*

CALLED TO ACTION

In the early 1800s, British ships began stopping American merchant ships from traveling to France. Thousands of American sailors were taken off vessels and forced to join the British navy. On June 18, 1812, the United States **declared** war on England.

The USS *Constitution* was called into action. As the frigate was trying to join the rest of the American navy, the crew found themselves being chased by five British warships! After more than 2 days, skillful **outmaneuvering** helped the *Constitution* outrun the British ships.

CREWMAN'S LOG

The British were gaining on us! Captain Hull told us to make the ship lighter, so we threw our drinking water overboard. We also wet the sails, which helped them catch light winds.

DURING THE WAR OF 1812, CAPTAIN ISAAC HULL COMMANDED THE USS *CONSTITUTION* AND ITS CREW OF MORE THAN 450 SAILORS.

OLD IRONSIDES

On August 19, 1812, the USS *Constitution* found itself against a British ship called HMS *Guerriere* near the coast of Nova Scotia, Canada. The British ship began to fire at the American vessel, but at least one cannonball just bounced off the *Constitution*! A sailor called out, "Her sides are made of iron!" The *Constitution* was often called Old Ironsides after this.

Then, the *Constitution* started firing back. About an hour later, the *Guerriere* surrendered, or gave up.

CREWMAN'S LOG

We were proud of our first victory over the British navy. We were greeted as heroes and were given $50,000 to split among us!

THE USS *CONSTITUTION* HAD 55 GUNS, WHILE THE HMS *GUERRIERE* HAD 38. THE *CONSTITUTION*'S CANNONBALLS WERE HEAVIER, WEIGHING 24 POUNDS (11 KG) EACH.

A CLASH WITH HMS JAVA

On December 29, 1812, the USS *Constitution* found itself south, near the coast of Brazil. Its orders were to "annoy the enemy." When it happened upon the British HMS *Java*, US captain William Bainbridge ordered his men to fire. A mighty battle followed as the ships got closer. The *Java* surrendered and soon sank.

After this, the British navy, at the time the strongest in the world, decided never to have its warships fight an American frigate one on one.

CREWMAN'S LOG

We had men up on the masts with guns firing at the sailors on the Java. The British captain, Henry Lambert, was killed by this gunfire.

CAPTAIN BAINBRIDGE WAS WOUNDED TWICE ON THE *CONSTITUTION*, BUT HE SURVIVED.

TWO AGAINST ONE

The War of 1812 ended February 17, 1815. The USS *Constitution* didn't know that when it met the HMS *Cyane* and HMS *Levant* near Spain on February 20, 1815. The *Constitution* fired and stopped to let the thick gun smoke clear. The *Levant* was next to it! The *Constitution* fired again, damaging the *Levant*.

The *Cyane* quickly came up on the *Constitution*'s stern, or rear. US captain Charles Stewart ordered his ship to sail back and fire at the *Cyane*. Both British ships finally surrendered to the *Constitution*.

CREWMAN'S LOG

We had to act fast when we saw the Levant next to us! The Levant took a bad blow from our guns and had to move away—allowing us to take on the Cyane.

THE BRITISH RECAPTURED THE HMS *LEVANT*, BUT THE HMS *CYANE* LATER BECAME PART OF THE US NAVY.

SAILING ON

The *Constitution* continued to serve the navy after the War of 1812. One of its missions was to capture ships off the coast of Africa that were illegally transporting slaves.

By 1830, the *Constitution* was in danger of being decommissioned. However, a popular poem by Oliver Wendell Holmes called "Old Ironsides" and a captain named John Percival stopped that from happening. "Mad Jack" Percival, the oldest of all the *Constitution*'s captains, took the ship on a world tour in the 1840s.

CREWMAN'S LOG

On our world tour, we mapped waters that were not yet explored officially by the United States. We stopped in Brazil, Singapore, Hong Kong, and Hawaii.

OLIVER WENDELL HOLMES'S POEM ARGUED THAT IT WOULD BE BETTER FOR THE MIGHTY *CONSTITUTION* TO SINK THAN BE TAKEN APART.

OLD IRONSIDES

Ay, tear her tattered ensign down!
Long has it waved on high,
And many an eye has danced to see
That banner in the sky;
Beneath it rung the battle shout,
And burst the cannon's roar;–
The meteor of the ocean air
Shall sweep the clouds no more!

Her deck, once red with heroes' blood
Where knelt the vanquished foe,
When winds were hurrying o'er the flood
And waves were white below,
No more shall feel the victor's tread,
Or know the conquered knee;–
The harpies of the shore shall pluck
The eagle of the sea!

O, better that her shattered hulk
Should sink beneath the wave;
Her thunders shook the mighty deep,
And there should be her grave;
Nail to the mast her holy flag,
Set every thread-bare sail,
And give her to the god of storms,–
The lightning and the gale!

TRAINING SHIP

In 1857, the *Constitution* was **refit** to be a training ship in Portsmouth, New Hampshire. When the American Civil War broke out in 1861, it was moved from Annapolis, Maryland, so that **Confederate** forces wouldn't capture it. The ship and the entire US Naval Academy went to Newport, Rhode Island. There, the *Constitution* was used to train the **Union** navy.

When the war ended in 1865, the *Constitution* returned to Annapolis. In the 1870s, the training ship was kept in Philadelphia, Pennsylvania.

CREWMAN'S LOG

We knew the Southern rebels would want our ship, so we sailed it out of the harbor. We got stuck! Luckily, another ship towed us, and we made our way north.

THIS PHOTOGRAPH, TAKEN IN 1858, IS THE FIRST KNOWN OF THE USS *CONSTITUTION*. IT SHOWS THE FRIGATE BEING REPAIRED.

MUSEUM SHIP

In 1931, the *Constitution* was towed on a tour of the United States. It stopped in 90 ports so Americans could celebrate its history. Then, it was returned to Boston, its birthplace.

In 2007, the USS *Constitution* underwent remodeling so it would look more like it did during the War of 1812. The frigate is now a museum ship in Boston that people can tour. Though no longer used in wars, this amazing ship is still a commissioned naval vessel with an important use.

CREWMAN'S LOG

As a US Navy sailor, I dreamed of sailing on this famous frigate. In 1997, the USS Constitution sailed by herself for the first time in 116 years—and I was on her!

THE USS *CONSTITUTION* IS TURNED AROUND EVERY YEAR IN BOSTON HARBOR.

GLOSSARY

bolt: a long, round piece of metal that has a wider part at one end and is like a screw at the other end

commission: to make officially active and ready for use

Confederate: having to do with the Confederate States of America formed by the Southern states during the American Civil War

declare: to say or state something in an official or public way

design: to create the pattern or shape of something

mission: a task or job a group must perform

outmaneuver: to use skill or cleverness to secure an advantage over someone

patriot: a person who loves and strongly supports or fights for his or her country

protection: the act of keeping safe

refit: to make a boat ready for use again, especially by adding new parts

Union: having to do with the side of the Northern states during the American Civil War

FOR MORE INFORMATION

Books

Boothroyd, Jennifer. *Inside the US Navy.* Minneapolis, MN: Lerner Publications, 2018.

Hamilton, John. *Frigates.* Minneapolis, MN: ABDO Publishing, 2012.

Rose, Simon. *The War of 1812.* New York, NY: AV2 by Weigl, 2015.

Websites

USS Constitution
www.nps.gov/bost/learn/historyculture/ussconst.htm
Read some facts about the ship, now in Boston, Massachusetts.

USS Constitution Museum
ussconstitutionmuseum.org
Check out the museum dedicated to this famous ship.

INDEX